MW01594876

JUST TALK TO JESUS

A THIRTY DAY DEVOTIONAL

Amy Jo Jezek

AMY JO JEZEK

JUST TALK
to
JESUS

A Thirty Day Devotional

B&B PUBLISHING GROUP

JUST TALK TO JESUS

Copyright © 2022 — Amy Jo Jezek

All rights reserved solely by the author. The author guarantees all contents are original and do not infringe upon the legal rights of any other person or work. No part of this book may be reproduced in any form without the permission of the author.

Unless otherwise indicated, Scripture taken from the New King James Version®. Copyright © 1982 by Thomas Nelson. Used by permission. All rights reserved.

ISBN: 9798366515726

B&B PUBLISHING GROUP

DEDICATIONS

Edward Jezek
Joshua & Brandon
Raegan & Xane

May prayer always be your portion.

One thing my father told me before he passed was I needed to write a book. After years of contemplating and chewing on it, not knowing where to start. I finally decided to just start somewhere.

When I began my search for Jesus, it was around 2004. I was searching for something MORE in my life. Change needed to come, and it had to start somewhere. The stories are long. Many failed relationships. Mothering two amazing sons. Figuring out how to support them, as well as myself, and work. Lots of wrong choices. The one thing I figured out was *Just Talk To Jesus.* He has the answer for everything. The answers will come, maybe not how we anticipate at times, but they will come. More than anything though, He longs to have a conversation with you. He longs for you to communicate with Him. It's the most important relationship you will ever have.

In September of 2005 I began writing emails and sending them out to an immediate group of friends, sharing my faith and including prayer in it. They began to share them with others, and 17 years later here we are. The prayers in this book are simply 30 days' worth of random prayers. I used to write every single morning and send them out. My encouragement and heart for this book is to help you in your journey to *Just*

Talk To Jesus. Talking to Him is free and never a dropped call or roaming charge. It's always unlimited. He's everywhere all the time. He never leaves you nor forsakes you. Just talk to Him.

People have said to me things like, "I don't know how to pray." "I don't know what to say." "You have a direct line to Jesus." Hearing this continues to fuel my passion to help others open their line of communication with our heavenly Father. I would encourage you to even read them aloud to help build your own faith, courage and confidence.

CONTENTS

Introduction

My heart is to help those who want to pray, but feel lost on what to say. It is to help open and establish communication with our Lord and Savior, Jesus Christ. It is to help you understand that prayer does not come with an expiration date. Prayer is free, simple and from the heart. Jesus paid the price for each and every one of us on Calvary's Cross over 2000 years ago. He longs for communication between us. Intimacy.

I purposefully left the dates on each prayer to show how on-time the Lord can be, regardless of when it was written. It also helps to see and understand how alive the Word of God (scripture) is. When you pick up the Word, it is able to speak to your heart at that very moment, regardless of when it was written. Prayer doesn't have to be elegant or elaborate; the Lord just longs for us to communicate with Him. He knows what's in our hearts — we do not need to try to hide it. We just need to take or make time to pray, to communicate — to simply have a conversation with the Lord.

My hope is to be able to jumpstart another's prayer life, and help them become more comfortable in talking to the Lord.

There is no specific order to the letters. I am praying for His grace to be sufficient in leading you.

The book was not designed to be read at once in its entirety, but rather as a devotional one day at a time, or simply as needed.

If this is all new to you, try to absorb a scripture or any scripture, and try not to complicate the simplicity of establishing open communication with the Lord. Just talk to Jesus. He loves you. He is for you. He is not against you. He will never leave you, nor forsake you, and is closer to you than a brother.

Blessings, my friends…

amy jo

Day 1 with Jesus

02DEC2020

Good Morning, Lord…

Thank You for making all things perfect in Your time. Help us to surrender our hearts to You. Keep our paths narrow and straight. Keep our steps in order and alignment to Your will and Your way. Every good gift and every perfect gift comes down from above — from You Father God.

Father, we know rebellion is as the sin of witchcraft and stubbornness is as iniquity and idolatry.

Both are blessing blockers, and cause one to be rejected from promotion or the seat they may hold. Saul was rejected from being king due to rebellion and stubbornness. Search our hearts, O Lord. Tear down the walls of stubbornness. Pull out the slivers of rebellion buried in our hearts. Help us to SURRENDER, and not be rejected, nor lose our seat.

We praise You, Father, for A MOVE. Let the winds of change begin to blow. Blow away reproach. Blow away stubbornness. Blow away rebellion. May we be quick to hear, slow to speak and slow to wrath. May we walk in obedience. May we "HEAR" and "OBEY." Obedience is better than sacrifice. May we TRUST You. May our TRUST rest IN YOU. May we TRUST knowing that ALL THINGS do work together for the good. May there be no dead, unfruitful, bitter or rotten branches left lingering. Help us to SURRENDER ALL. May we rise up and put on our garments of PRAISE. We thank You for giving us beauty where there were once ashes. We thank You for pouring out the oil of JOY where we once mourned. Establish our steps. Align our calendars and appointments with Your perfect will. May it be Your will and Your plans, and not our own. Give us this day our daily bread. Your provisions are always perfect.

(Psalm 94:20) May the throne of iniquity have no fellowship with us.

We shall trust in the Lord, and do good; Dwell in the land and feed on Your faithfulness Father God. We shall delight ourselves in You. We shall trust You to give us the desires of our heart, because You put them there. Remove our thinking and replace it with Yours. Your ways are higher Your thoughts are not our thoughts. We shall commit our ways to You. We shall trust You. We shall rest knowing You will bring it to pass. You order our steps. Help us to delight in Your ways. When we keep Your ways, You exalt us to inherit the land.

Cover all connected to or concerning us in the mighty blood of Jesus Bless and protect our children, and our children's children. Establish our steps.

In Jesus' name, amen.

Your Thoughts and Reflections:

Roman 12:2

Day 2 with Jesus

03NOV2020

Good Morning, Lord…

Thank You for this beautiful day, this beautiful WEEK. Thank You that what You have blessed no man can curse. Let us not curse ourselves. We praise You for the establishment of kingdom order being fulfilled today. We praise You for the army of the Lord rising up and taking their stand. We praise You for Your hand continually being upon us. You are gracious. You are merciful. We are ever humbled by Your presence.

We praise You today for <u>Psalm 91:11. He shall give His angels charge over us to keep us</u> in all of our ways.

Thank You Lord for those appointed, anointed and assigned to keep us in all of our ways. Your people. Your placement. Your leadership. Those of the Kingdom of God — the Kingdom of Heaven. Let it be on earth as it is in heaven. ESTABLISH IT THIS DAY.

We praise You for 2 Chronicles 20:20.

"…Believe in the Lord your God, and you shall be established;
believe His prophets, and you shall prosper."
vs.21 "...Praise the Lord, For His mercy endures forever."
vs.22 "Now when they began to sing and to praise, the Lord set
ambushes against the people of Ammon, Moab, and Mount Seir, who
had come against Judah; and they were defeated."

Lord, we are crying out to You this morning for Your governmental order to be ESTABLISHED. We praise You for Your mercy enduring forever. We are believing and trusting Your words, Your voice being heard in the land. We are believing to prosper. We are praising You that Your people shall be victorious this day.

We praise You for beauty for the ashes. We praise You for the NEW thing You are doing. We praise You for the ways being made where there seemed to be no way. We praise You for working all things out together for the good. We praise You for delivering us. We praise You for touching our lips and giving us the words to speak. We praise You for Jeremiah 1. We praise You for speaking the words You command. We praise You that You, Lord, shall prevail. You are with us. You are our deliverer. We put You in remembrance.

We praise You today for COMPLETE healing. No more shall our vision be distorted. No more shall we see "men like trees" but rather we shall see CLEARLY. PERFECT VISION is coming into fullness and completeness. We praise You for the gift of discernment. We praise You for leading, guiding and directing us on when and whom to speak to or not. We praise You for the STRUCTURAL ALIGNMENT that is being corrected and established. We give You all the praise and glory this day. We praise You that our praise releases confusion to the enemy. Our praise is able to cause the enemies to come against one another. We praise You this battle is not ours, but Yours Lord. We only need to continue to lift our praise — to sing, to shout and to bless. We lift up our praise to You this day. Victory belongs to You Lord. Let the Glory of the Lord fill the house.

Cover all connected to or concerning us in the mighty blood of Jesus. We pray for Spiritual Wisdom this day Lord. Let spiritual wisdom be released throughout our land and among Your people.

(Ephesians 1:15-22) "Therefore I also, after I heard of your faith in the Lord Jesus and your love for all the saints, do not cease to give thanks for you, making mention of you in my prayers: that the God of our Lord Jesus Christ, the Father of glory, may give to you the spirit of wisdom and revelation in the knowledge of Him, the eyes of your understanding being enlightened; that you may know what is the hope of His calling, what are the riches of the glory of His

inheritance in the saints, and what is the exceeding greatness of His power toward us who believe, according to the working of His mighty power which He worked in Christ when He raised Him from the dead and seated Him at His right hand in the heavenly places, far above all principality and power and might and dominion, and every name that is named, not only in this age but also in that which is to come. And He put all things under His feet, and gave Him to be head over all things to the church, which is His body, the fullness of Him who fills all in all."

In Jesus' name, amen.

Your Thoughts and Reflections:

Day 3 with Jesus

05NOV2020

Good Morning, Lord...

Thank You for Fall, and all the beautiful colors. You paint such beautiful pictures. You are truly majestic. Thank You for Romans 8:28. We praise You for working all things out together for the good for those who love You, and are called according to Your purpose. You are a God of Divine Orchestration. Holy, holy, holy is the Lord God Almighty.

This month, we shall continue to praise You for Psalm 91:11. That Your angels are set charge over us to keep us in all of our ways. Holy, holy, holy is the Lord God Almighty. Let everything that has a voice praise the Lord.

We praise You for Romans 8:31, knowing that if You are for us, then who can be against us? We praise You for MORE being for us than there are against us.

We shall continue to lift up our praise to You, O Lord, as You instructed them in 2 Chronicles 20:20-22. We shall believe in You, knowing You will establish us. We shall believe Your prophets, knowing we shall prosper. We shall praise You, knowing Your mercy does endure forever. We shall praise You, knowing our praise is the weapon of our warfare. We shall continue to praise You in all things. We praise You, knowing all things are possible with and through You. You are the Great God Almighty, and You have never lost a battle.

Bless the work of our hands this day. Thank You that You continue to restructure, realign and reassign. You continue to reappoint and reseat. May no one put their mouths to Your anointed. Thank You for divine appointments today. Thank You that You have already orchestrated our day as we surrender it to You. Establish our steps. Lead, guide and direct us. May we only speak the words You give us. We cancel out the assignments and fiery darts of the enemy sent against us and our loved ones. Cover all connected to or concerning us in the mighty blood of Jesus. Thank You for the veil being torn. Thank You for the shed blood at Calvary. Thank You for being the God of Restoration. Our hope and our trust is in You, O Lord.

In Jesus' name, amen.

Your Thoughts and Reflections:

Day 4 with Jesus

10DEC2020

Good Morning, Lord…

Thank You for waking us up early, and time spent with You. Thank You for Your word, and Your voice being the truth and the light. Whom the Son sets free is free indeed. Thank You for freedom. Freeing us from those things that so easily beset us. Thank You that it is Your desire that our joy be made full. Full of You. Your good and perfect gifts come from above, and in You there is not even a shadow of darkness. Thank You for Your powerful prayer warriors in whom Your word is deeply planted.

Thank You for REVELATION KNOWLEDGE being poured out even this day. Thank You for EXTRACTING the LIES. Thank You for DOWNLOADING the TRUTH into our hearts, minds, soul, body and spirit THIS DAY. For whom the Son sets FREE is FREE INDEED. Freedom from the lies that were ingrained in us, even as far back as birth and / or childhood. Extract the lies and let the TRUTH be received.

How do we know what the TRUTH is?

(1 John 1:5-10) "This is the message that we have heard from Him and declare to you, that God is light and in Him is no darkness at all. If we say that we have fellowship with Him, and walk in darkness, we lie and do not practice the truth. But if we walk in the light as He is in the light, we have fellowship with one another, and the blood of Jesus Christ His Son cleanses us from all sin. If we say that we have no sin, we deceive ourselves, and the truth is not in us. If we confess our sins, He is faithful and just to forgive us our sins and to cleanse us from all unrighteousness. If we say that we have not sinned, we make Him a liar, and His word is not in us."

Lord, we have been in a place of REFORMATION. In reforming us, You purify and sanctify us. You wash us and cleanse us. Help us to cleanse ourselves. Help us to abstain from all unrighteousness. Keep us in Your will, walking in Your ways, on Your path. Cover all connected to or concerning us in the mighty blood of Jesus. Thank You for the work You are doing in families, Lord. Thank You for alignment and restoration. REBUILDING, REJUVENATING and REFORTIFYING. You are the great God Jehovah. Merciful, mighty, greatly to be praised!

Bless the work of our hands that we may be fruitful, multiplying and subduing the land. Bless and protect our children and our children's children. Thank You for grace. Thank You that goodness and mercy are following us all of our days. Thank You that when all of our tithes are brought into the storehouse — You do rebuke the devourer for our sakes. You will open the windows of heaven that we may not have room enough to receive. We have never seen the righteous forsaken nor his seed begging bread. You are the God of more than enough. Exceedingly, abundantly above and beyond what we could ask or think.

In Jesus' name, amen.

Your Thoughts and Reflections:

Day 5 with Jesus

02FEB2021

Good Morning, Lord...

Thank You for this fresh brisk morning! You are God, and You are amazing! We shall love You with all our heart, all our soul and all our mind. In You and with You, all things are possible. Thank You that when we search for you with ALL of our heart — we find YOU. You are wonderful, holy, counselor and King. Nothing shall be impossible for You. You, God, are not out of options! Hallelujah! That is what You do — You keep on coming through. Thank You that success doesn't always come through the first attempt. Thank You for a fresh breath, a fresh strength, a fresh new anointing to rise up and run this race set before us. We shall not grow weary. We shall not faint. We shall rise up with wings like eagles. We shall rise above what we see, and move to higher heights for clearer visibility. Thank You for clearing our vision. Help us to see what You see. Unclog our deaf ears to hear fully what You are saying.

Thank You for the power of the Holy Spirit dwelling within us — here with us. Thank You the Holy Spirit is peace, joy, love, gentleness, righteousness, kindness, longsuffering, goodness & self-control. Thank You we are able to call forth the Holy Spirit in us to help us through situations that present themselves in our lives. When we are unsure or unstable - we call forth these things. When doubt creeps in or fear tries to gain control, we call forth the Holy Spirit within us, and decree power, love and a sound mind. We call forth the fruits of the Spirit into our situations and surroundings. We call forth the peace of God which surpasses all understanding. We call forth righteousness when unrighteousness is present. We praise You for kindness, gentleness and self-control coming forth when things look the

13

opposite. We thank You today for the kingdom of heaven being AT HAND, and the Holy Spirit dwelling within us.

Bless the work of our hands today. May we be fruitful, multiply and subdue the land. May we possess the land everywhere the soles of our feet tread for kingdom's sake and kingdom purpose to glorify You Lord. We praise You for continually rearranging schedules, calendars and appointments so that we are not out of kingdom order. May no divine appointment be missed. We praise You that even today we shall entertain angels. We praise You today that we will not forsake the fellowship of the saints. We thank You that You do work all things out for the good for those who love You, and are the called according to Your purpose in Christ Jesus. We thank You for the blood of Jesus covering everything connected to or concerning us. We thank You for protecting and providing for each of us, and our children & children's children. We praise You our steps are ordered by You. We are blessed going in and blessed coming out. We return to You Your portion of all You bless us with, and give us charge or stewardship over. You are the Great God Jehovah — our Provider. You are Jehovah Rapha and Jehovah Nissi. Your banner over us is LOVE.

In Jesus' name, amen.

Your Thoughts and Reflections:

Day 6 with Jesus

11NOV2020

Good Morning, Lord!

Thank You the sun is shining! It's cool, crisp & beautiful! You truly make all things beautiful in Your time! Righteous and holy are thee O King. Thank You for Psalm 92 this morning! You are so amazing! Yes, it is good to give thanks to the Lord and sing praises to Your name! To declare Your lovingkindness in the morning, and Your faithfulness at night. You are on high forevermore. Thank You for anointing us with fresh oil! Thank You the righteous shall flourish like the palm tree. Thank You for those planted in Your house, flourishing in Your courts. Thank You they will still bear fruit in old age, and shall be fresh and flourishing! You are our Rock! There is no unrighteousness in You Lord!

Lord, this morning let us bring those battling sickness, infirmities or disease before You. We command every spirit of infirmity, sickness or disease coming against Your people to flee. Every name must bow to the name of Jesus. We are warriors in agreement standing united, locked in arms, fighting and believing for Your people.

We call forth a recovery of all that has been lost! Health, time, broken families or finances.

We are standing agreed FOR SWIFT RETURNS! 7 FOLD RETURNS to begin right now.

The thief has been found out therefore we praise You for the returns beginning RIGHT NOW.

SUPERNATURAL RETURNS right to our doorstep!

Let everyone shout RETURN! RETURN! RETURN!

JESUS! YOU ARE THE AUTHOR & FINISHER OF OUR FAITH! It is our FAITH that MAKES US WELL!

We are calling out the little foxes that have been spoiling our vines! I believe there was an old movie called "To Catch a Thief." This has been on my mind the past 24 hours. Catching the little foxes that are robbing, stealing or pilfering our time and resources.

Catch the little foxes Lord! Reveal, expose, pluck up, pull out, cast off all that was working against us and bring on the RETURNS! HALLELUJAH JESUS!

We praise you for supernatural REST and RECOVERY OF ALL. We praise you for actual time to communicate. Clear communication. No misinterpretations. No disruptions. We praise you for all things being made beautiful in your time.

We praise you for other mighty warriors You have raised up! Oh, how it blesses my soul when they jump in fired up for you Lord! Oh, how we praise you. Oh, how you love us!

Thank You for covering all that is connected or concerning us in the mighty blood of Jesus. Thank You that no weapons formed against us shall prosper. Thank You for Your angels set charge over us, keeping us in all of our ways. Thank You for time well spent, calendars set in Your perfect order, divine alignments, assignments and appointments this day. Thank You there is MUCH SHIFTING. ALIGNMENT and CHANGE happening. We praise you for supernatural GRACE, MERCY AND MOVEMENT in each of our lives. We praise you for DIVINE FAVOR resting on each one of us as well as our family members.

In Jesus' mighty name, AMEN!

Your Thoughts and Reflections:

Day 7 with Jesus

23NOV2020

Good Morning, Lord…

Thank You for yet another beautiful day. Your ways are righteous. Your ways are pure. Your ways are holy. Holy, holy, holy is the great God Almighty. Thank You we have never seen the righteous forsaken, nor his seed begging bread. There are no beggars in the kingdom, for You know every need. There is no want nor lack, because You provide exceedingly abundantly above and beyond all we could ask, think or even yet imagine. You divinely orchestrate our days, our paths, our schedules, calendars and appointments. Thank You for always being the way maker and chain breaker. You make roads in the wilderness and rivers in the desert. Your thoughts are not our thoughts, nor are Your ways our ways. We thank You that they are always so much higher. How awesome is our God. You are the Good Shepherd, always going before us. You are the Gentlemen who opens all of the doors that You have set before us. You shield us. You guard us. You protect us. You are the Lover of our souls. You give us wisdom and knowledge. The ability to get wealth, and to prosper, comes directly from You. All things are from You, and FOR YOU. Let all we do be unto You. Thank You for Your favor resting upon us.

Thank You that not only do You open Your doors, but You lock the doors that are not of You that we may not enter in. What You lock, no man can open. What You open, no man can shut. For that, we praise You. We send up our praise to You today. Our praise goes out before us. Our praise is a weapon. This is how we fight our battle — by merely praising You. Thank You for loving us anyway. You love us in spite of our seemingly wretched selves. You love us when we are unable to love ourselves. You love us in spite of how ugly our past may have been. You are the lifter of our heads. The wind beneath our wings You cause us to run and not be weary; to walk and not faint. Our hope and our trust is in You O Lord. Thank You for all You have done and are doing. Thank You Your yoke is easy and Your burden is light. Thank You we are able to cast all of our cares on You, for You care for us. Thank You that this day, we shall take up our bed and walk. Thank You we shall have peace in our heart. Perfect peace comes from You, and surpasses all understanding. Our hope, our trust is in You Lord. Your ways are perfect. Thank You for blessing and protecting our children, and our children's children. Thank You for unknown sources and supernatural provision. You love obedience more than sacrifice. Help us to walk humbly before You. Thank You for our daily provisions. Thank You for Your hand continually upon us — may we not cause pain. Bless us indeed, O Lord. Bless us indeed. Perfect order to our day. Divine appointments in place. Your angels charge over us. Cover all connected to or concerning us in the mighty blood of Jesus.

In Jesus' name, amen.

Your Thoughts and Reflections:

Day 8 with Jesus

31MAR2019

Good Morning, Lord!

Praise God for sunshine! Hallelujah!

Praise God for promotion and increase. Though we may not understand — though it may not be tangibly in our hand — Praise God it is NEAR. It is on the HORIZON.

(Zechariah 4:6) "...This is the word of the Lord to Zerubbabel: "Not by might nor by power, but by My Spirit,' Says the Lord of hosts."

Thank You it is the rain that brings the INCREASE. It is the rain that washes away all impurities. It is the rain that brings the cleansing and healing. Praise God for the former and the latter rain.

Thank You we are moving into a season of EXPANSION and ENLARGEMENT. INCREASE and PROMOTION are coming. Glory be Your name, O Lord.

Thank You we walk by faith, and not by sight. It is our faith that moves mountains. It is our faith that makes us whole. It is by faith promises are obtained and fulfilled. Thank You that we are able to call those things that be not as though they are. Thank You for the seers, and those crying out in the wilderness.

Lord, thank You today for "REBRANDING" us. Pour out creativity and witty inventions. Debt cancellation. Forgiveness in every arena. Forgive us our debts as we forgive our debtors. Lead us not into temptation, but deliver us from the evil one. Thank You DELIVERANCE has come. Thank You for doing all we are not able to do on our own. We give it all to You, O God. You are able to cause rivers in the desert. The blind to see. The lame to walk. The deaf to hear. The dead to raise. We release all we are holding onto into Your hands. Blessed be Your name.

Thank You that just as the loaves and fishes were released to You, You BLESSED them, You BROKE them, then You MULTIPLIED them. Once blessed and broken — then increase and multiplication can come. Thank You for "breaking us" O Lord. Causing us to let go of ourselves; our natural thinking that we can and are able to do it on our own. Thank God for surrender and release.

Cover all connected to or concerning us in the blood of Jesus. Bless and protect our children, and our children's children. Get us where You would have us to be, and see whom You would have us to see this day.

In Jesus' name, amen.

Your Thoughts and Reflections:

Day 9 with Jesus

08FEB2021

Good Morning, Lord...

Thank You for a complete day of REST. Thank You we are in a time of reformation and transformation. Thank You for returning our focus to being obedient to You. There is no wiggle room in obedience. We can come to You by faith, but we can only grow by obedience. Thank You simple obedience produces great rewards. Thank You our victory is In Jesus' Name.

Thank You that it all begins in a place of prayer. Thank You for purifying our motives, Lord. Thank You Lord for helping us to build our house, and not be foolish. (Prov.14:1) Thank You the king's heart is in Your hand, and like rivers of water flow, You turn it whatever way You wish. (Prov.21:1) Thank You for plucking up and uprooting every wicked, unhealthy or unwholesome thing in our lives, homes, families, workplaces & this nation!

(Jeremiah 33:3) says, "Call to Me, and I will answer you, and show you great and mighty things, which you do not know."

Thank You for revealing those things we do not know — even the great and mighty things — those things beyond our present understanding. We shall see a victory — the battle belongs to You, Lord. Show us Your plan, and not our own. Show us Your supply, and not the supply we would attempt to muster up. Show us what these things look like according to YOUR WILL. Refresh our vision. Heal our eyes and unclog deaf ears. Thy will be done.

(Jeremiah 32:17) "Ah, Lord God! Behold, You have made the heavens and the earth by Your great power and outstretched arm. There is nothing too hard for You."

(Isaiah 43:18,19) "'Do not remember the former things, Nor consider the things of old. Behold, I will do a new thing, Now it shall spring forth; Shall you not know it? I will even make a road in the wilderness And rivers in the desert."

vs.26 "Put Me in remembrance; Let us contend together; State your case, that you may be acquitted." A synonym for acquitted is FREE.

(John 8:36) "Therefore if the Son makes you free, you shall be free indeed."

Acquit means: to relieve from a charge of fault or crime; declare not guilty; to release or discharge (a person) from an obligation; to settle or satisfy (a debt, obligation, claim, etc.); to bear or conduct (oneself); behave; to free or clear (oneself). (Dictionary.com)

Lord, help us to recognize and expose the lies of the enemy, the father of lies, and replace them with Your truth, Your word...the word of God.

Lord, order our steps today. The steps of the righteous are ordered by the Lord. Bless the work of our hands that we may be fruitful, multiply and subdue the land. Change, change and rearrange anything out of Your divine order. Align our schedules, calendars and appointments with Your will, way and divine timing. Set us in Your order. Set us up for a divine set up. Righteous and holy are thee, O King. Send us who we need to see today, and who needs to see us. Thank You for divine appointments, divine orchestration and heavenly provisions. Thy kingdom come. Thy will be done. On earth as it is in heaven. Thank You that even today we shall entertain angels. Thank You for the Holy Spirit dwelling among us. Thank You it takes faith to be faithful. Thank You mountains are moved with a mustard seed of faith. Lord, we believe, but help us with any unbelief we may be experiencing. May we not be busybodies, but about Your business. Cover all connected to or concerning us in the mighty blood of Jesus. Thank You it is well with my soul. Bless and protect our children, and our children's children. Thank You for restoring every heart that is broken.

In Jesus' name, amen.

Your Thoughts and Reflections:

Day 10 with Jesus

26JAN21

Good Morning, Lord…

Help us to come back to what really matters: YOU. Nothing else will do. Rend our hearts, and not our garments. Lord, help us to pull aside and gather all we've gone through. Help us to be still, and enter into rest. Rest & Evaluation. Help us to press into rest that we may hear Your still small voice. Help us to hear the wind. Help us to discern the wind. The wind of the Holy Spirit. We know it is not by might, nor by power, but by Your Spirit that mountains are moved. (Zech.4:6) It is through You the impossible becomes possible. Help us to discern the times and seasons. Help us to discern the greater purpose at hand. Water us Lord. Send Your REFRESHMENT. Not the refreshing we think we need or would seek out on our own, but the refreshment of YOU. Give us a drink Lord.

(Matthew 5:6) "Blessed are those who hunger and thirst for righteousness, For they shall be filled."

(Jeremiah 29:13) "And you will seek Me and find Me, when you search for Me with all your heart."

(Joel 2:12,13) "'Now, therefore,' says the Lord, 'Turn to Me with all your heart, With fasting, with weeping, and with mourning.' So rend your heart, and not your garments; Return to the Lord your God, For He is gracious and merciful, Slow to anger, and of great kindness; And He relents from doing harm."

Lord, meet us at the well. The Well of REFRESHING for our VICTORY is in JESUS name. He is our rock, our fortress, our strong tower. Our present help in times of trouble. Our REDEEMER.

(Hosea 2:16) "'And it shall be, in that day,' Says the Lord, 'That you will call Me 'My Husband,' and no longer call Me 'My Master', For I will take from her mouth the names of the Baals, And they shall be remembered by their name no more.'"

The Lord is removing the things that stand between our heart and His. He is tearing down the golden calves, and places of idolatry & adultery towards Him. He is the one true source and provider.

(Hosea 2:19) "'I will betroth you to Me forever; Yes, I will betroth you to Me In righteousness and justice, In lovingkindness and mercy; I will betroth you to Me in faithfulness, And you shall know the Lord."

Lord, help us to know You more. Help us to rend our hearts to You. You desire obedience more than sacrifice. Help us O Lord. Have mercy on us.

Thank You today for unexpected blessings. Thank You the waters parted, and the Red Sea swallowed the pursuants. Thank You the weapons of our warfare are not carnal, but mighty in God for pulling down strongholds, casting down arguments, and every high thing that exalts itself against the knowledge of God, bringing every thought into captivity to the obedience of Christ, and being ready to punish all disobedience when your obedience is fulfilled. (2 Corin. 10:4-6)

Lord, change, change and rearrange everything not in alignment or accordance to Your will and Your way. Set us in Your order. Help us to BE STILL and KNOW. Pour out Godly Wisdom, knowledge and clear direction. Let us set our face like a flint towards You. It is You we seek, Your knowledge, Your will, Your way. May it be ON EARTH as it is in heaven. Give us THIS DAY our DAILY BREAD. Lead us not into temptation but deliver us from the evil one. Enlarge our territories. Stretch out the curtains of our dwellings. Let FAITH arise. Our hope and trust is in You, O Lord. Cover all connected to or concerning us in the mighty blood of Jesus.

Thank You for plucking out the little foxes that spoil the vine Close up the entry ways where any pestilence has entered. Take out the trash. Clear the clutter. Send the deliverer. Bless the work of our hands. Thank You we are lenders and not borrowers.

In Jesus' mighty name, amen.

Your Thoughts and Reflections:

Day 11 with Jesus

20MAR19

Good Morning, Lord…

Thank You for VICTORY! The first place You took me was Psalm 129, "A Song of Victory over Zion's Enemies." In our warfare we have been fighting for the victory. Praise You the VICTORY has come. The VICTORY is ours.

> *(Psalm 129: 1, 2) "'Many a time they have afflicted me from my youth…'" Let Israel now say: "Many a time they have afflicted me from my youth; Yet they have not prevailed against me."*

> *(Deut. 32:35) "'Vengeance is Mine, and recompense; Their foot shall slip in due time; For the day of their calamity is at hand, And the things to come hasten upon them.'"*

Lord, thank You the affairs of this land are on Your mind. Thank You for the power of praise. Thank You that when we keep our mind stayed on You; You wage the war for us. Thank You that we cannot serve two masters. Thank You for being a jealous God, a loving Father, and an all consuming fire. Mighty is Your name. Thank You for the rain bringing the cleansing & the healing in this land this day. Removing the stench. Removing iniquities. Let everyone that hath a breath praise the Lord. Thank You for the dry bones rising. Thank You for the army of heaven rising up. Let us raise a hallelujah in the presence of our enemies. God, You alone, are glorious and wonderful. You are our strength, strong tower, present help in times of trouble. Our provider, Jehovah Jireh. El Shadai.

Lord, as we go about this day, let our focus remain on "What is pleasing to YOU." May we not be people pleasers, men pleasers, but pleasing to the Most High God. Thank You it doesn't have to make sense to others, only to You. May

PEACE have it's portion. May PEACE lead our day. Chaos and confusion is not of You. Let every decision be made in PEACE. If there is no presence of PEACE; then do not go that way. Turnaround. Be still and wait.

Cover all connected to or concerning us in the blood of Jesus. Order our schedule, align our appointments and calendars to match up with Your perfect will. Cancel out anything not that is not pleasing You. Cancel out the plans of man and set us on Your path. Lead the way! Bless the work of our hands that we would be fruitful, multiplying and possessing the land You have called us too.

In the mighty name of Jesus, amen.

Your Thoughts and Reflections:

Day 12 with Jesus

26MAR2019

Good Morning, Lord…

Blessed be the name of the Lord. You, Lord, are righteous, merciful and holy. You are ever-loving. Thank You that it is not Your will that any man should perish. Lord, thank You that Your heart is for the lost, the broken and the prodigals. Your arms are always extended, "O sinner…come home." Praise God for grace. New measures of grace being poured out daily. Thank You that we walk by faith and not by sight.

> *(Daniel 10:12) "Then he said to me, 'Do not fear, Daniel, for from the first day that you set your heart to understand, and to humble yourself before your God, your words were heard; and I have come because of your words.*
>
> *vs.13 'But the prince of the kingdom of Persia withstood me twenty-one days; and behold, Michael, one of the chief princes, came to help me, for I had been left alone there with the kings of Persia.*
>
> *vs.14 'Now I have come to make you understand what will happen to your people in the latter days, for the vision refers to many days yet to come.'"*

Have you ever considered but for a moment that your prayer WAS HEARD but your calling, your vision, is such a threat to the kingdom, all hell broke loose to stop it?

Have you ever considered the battle against you isn't personal, but attached to the lives of those who will be impacted for the kingdom?

Have you ever considered that what you do DOES matter?

Are you thinking BIGGER than you? Is your dream or vision BIGGER than just YOU. Does it affect the lives of others? Does it bring change & kingdom growth? Is it generational?

Then RAISE A HALLELUJAH for the battle that has raged against you. The battle belongs to the Lord. Praise God for lives touched and souls saved.

Father, forgive us for being so caught up in ourselves that we lost sight of the kingdom impact at hand. Forgive us of our sins. Forgive us for being self-centered, selfish and "all about me." Lord, we call in the lost sheep. We dispatch the angels on assignment now. Turn them O Lord. Turn each of us from our wicked ways. Stand us upright O Lord. Move US out of the way, Lord. May we humble ourselves under the mighty hand of God.

You are the God that restores. You heal the broken-hearted, and bind up all their wounds. You set the captives free. Blessed be the name of the Lord. Lord, for we know now the enemy has been found out. Let the double portion begin to flow — the wells have been unlocked.

(Zechariah 9:12) "'Return to the stronghold, You prisoners of hope. Even today I declare That I will restore double to you.'"

Cover all connected to or concerning us in the blood of Jesus. God, we give You all the glory.

In Jesus' name, amen.

Your Thoughts and Reflections:

Day 13 with Jesus

25MAR19

Good Morning, Lord…

Praise God for this cold, windy, wet day. Let everything that hath breath Praise The Lord.

Lord, Your word says we serve the God of the Impossible. You cause the blind to see; the deaf to hear; the lame to walk; the dead to rise. You give us beauty for ashes. The oil of Joy for the spirit of heaviness. You are near to the brokenhearted. You are the repairer of the breach. You are the restorer of the streets. You make crooked places straight. You can make dry bones live.

We are above and not beneath. We are the head and not the tail. You are our provider… Jehovah Jireh. Lord, let us not forget all the miracles You have ALREADY done. Praise God for the testimonies You have given us. Thank You that when our faith is weary, we can reach in the box and pull out our reminders of how faithful You always are.

Lord, You returned a laptop stolen in Marion County when no one thought it was possible. You returned a cell phone stolen in Daytona Beach when others didn't believe it was possible. You provided all that was needed to bring the bills up to date when my job was not nearly enough. You have restored broken lines of communication. You cause gas cards to manifest when the tank was on E.

Lord, You said we are given a measure of faith. It is our faith that makes us well. It is our faith that makes us whole. It is by faith we are saved. I know our faith has been tested. I am so thankful for our intercessors. I am thankful it is always darkest right before the dawn. I am thankful Lazarus was dead for 4 days, so that all who saw it knew only the Lord could do such a thing.

Thank You that we are about to see Your glory come forth. We are about to see the glory manifest. Thank You for eye opening; jaw dropping moments. Thank You we shall come out of the fire without a stench of smoke. Thank You that when the waters felt like they would overtake us, You never let us drown.

Thank You for Your perfect will. Great grace. A new measure of faith to push the rest of the way through.

Lord, cover all connected to or concerning us in the blood of Jesus. Order our steps. Change, change and rearrange our calendars and appointments to line up with Your will. Get us where we need to be to see who we need to see.

In Jesus' name, amen.

Your Thoughts and Reflections:

Day 14 with Jesus

21MAR19

Good Morning, Lord!

Thank You for Amos 3:7: *"Surely the Lord God does nothing, Unless He reveals His secret to His servants, the prophets."*

Lord, thank You for the prophets. Those who set their heart to seek and hear Your voice. To hear the word of the Lord. Thank You for perfect timing. Your timing.

(Isaiah 55:8,9) "'For My thoughts are not your thoughts, Nor are your ways My ways,' says the Lord, 'For as the heavens are higher than the earth, So are My ways higher than your ways, And My thoughts than your thoughts."

(Habakkuk 2:2-4) "Then the Lord answered me and said: 'Write the vision And make it plain on tablets, That he may run who reads it. For the vision is yet for an appointed time; But at the end it will speak, and it will not lie. Though it tarries, wait for it; Because it will surely come, It will not tarry. 'Behold the proud, His soul is not upright in him; But the just shall live by his faith."

Lord, You are Mighty and All-Knowing. You know the end from the beginning. Thank You for appointed times and seasons, stretching, grooming and growing us. Faithful are You, O Lord. Bless the work of our hands that we may always be fruitful, multiplying and subduing the land. Thank You for being the good shepherd who always goes out ahead of us clearing the path, clearing away the debris. Free the path from destruction. Free the path from that which would lie in wait trying to rob, steal, kill and destroy the assignment You have for us. Blessed be Your name, O God. Thank You for unity, like-mindedness, complimenting relationships and friendships. Thank You for that which builds us up and does not tear us down. Open our eyes to see as You would see. Unclog our deafened ears. Break up the fallow ground in our hardened hearts. Let us seek ye first the kingdom and trust that all else will be provided THIS DAY. Cover all connected to or concerning us in the blood of Jesus.

In Jesus' name, amen.

Your Thoughts and Reflections:

Day 15 with Jesus

27JAN21

Good Morning, Lord…

Thank You for this beautiful day. This is the day the Lord hath made, and we shall rejoice in it. Again, thank You for 2 Corinthians 10:3-6:

For though we walk in the flesh, we do not war according to the flesh. For the weapons of our warfare are not carnal, but mighty in God for pulling down strongholds, casting down arguments and every high thing that exalts itself against the knowledge of God, bringing every thought into captivity to the obedience of Christ, and being ready to punish all disobedience when your obedience is fulfilled."

Countless times throughout the word of God You have shown us this. Jehoshaphat had three armies come against him. As he sought YOU first, the instruct ions You released to him were simple; RELEASE PRAISE. STAND STILL. DO NOT FEAR. The battle is the Lords.

If you are not familiar with this, read 2 Chronicles 20. There are keys released in it to help us know how to stand even now. Seek the Lord first. Gather together and ask the Lord for help. Fast. Do not be afraid nor dismayed because of this great multitude, for the battle is not yours, but God's. Position yourselves. Stand still. Believe in the Lord your God, and you shall be established. Believe His prophets, and you shall prosper. Appoint those to sing and who should praise the beauty of His holiness. "Praise the Lord, for His mercy endures forever." As they did the Lord set ambushes against the people of Ammon, Moab, and Mount Seir…..to the point they helped destroy one another.

There are several times throughout the word that the Lord won the battles without the people waging war. He simply required some form of worship / obedience from them. The four lepers at the gate. They could stay there and die, or get up with courage and faith and go forward. Once they did, the enemy had been defeated before they got there. In Nehemiah, he was granted permission by the king to go and rebuild, then here came three (yes, 3) against their work. The king had already given the decrees, the commands, for all resources needed to be released for the rebuilding of the city, and up rose the voices to come against the work that the Lord had approved. Now, here we are, our nation was being rebuilt and... bam! So, what would You think the Lord would have us to do? PRAISE HIM. Even when the Israelites were leaving Egypt, every time Moses went to Pharaoh it got worse. The Lord was after Pharaoh. Yes, he was dealing with the Israelites, but the Lord was after Pharaoh. What is required of us — OBEDIENCE. Praise, Worship, set our faces to seek the Lord, and not look at the things standing between Him and us. Rend our HEARTS. Allow Him to remove those things that are in the way of our relationship with Him. Stop looking at the mess, and get Your eyes on Him. Ask Him to search you. Ask Him to create in You a clean heart Ask Him to rearrange Your day in accordance to His Will, and not Your own. Ask Him to keep you from evil. Ask Him to keep you from temptation — and when He makes a way of escape — TAKE IT, rather than conceding to the temptation. Know your limit. Know when to say when, or simply do not put yourself in the position. Surrender your heart to Him, and let Him fight the battle for you.

Lord, cover all that is connected to or concerning us in mighty blood of Jesus. Search the hearts of man today. Man looks at the outward appearance, but You Lord know every intent of the heart. Create in us clean hearts. Send the rain, Lord. Send the rain. Let Your healing rain flow across this land, across this nation. May hearts return to You Lord. Bless the work of our hands. Thank You that every need has already been met. Every supply is on the way, it has already been released. Thank

You that we shall see Satan fall like lightning. We praise You for a clean sweep — in our hearts, in our homes and in this nation.

In Jesus' name, amen.

Your Thoughts and Reflections:

Day 16 with Jesus

17NOV2020

Good Morning, Lord…

Help us to rend our hearts, and not our garments. May we walk humbly before You. Forgive us our sins, the sins of this nation, the sins of our forefathers, those who have gone before us. Thank You for divine order, and the restructuring You have been doing. Realigning and reassigning. Let us be glad and rejoice. Let us continually praise You in the gates. Let us enter into Your presence with praise and thanksgiving. We thank You that praise is a weapon. We praise You we are not wrestling flesh and blood, but principalities and powers that rule in the darkness. We praise You for the remnant. We praise You that You allow us to be a blessing to others. We are blessed to be a blessing.Thank You for the opportunities to lend unto You. Keep our mind stayed on You. Keep our days in alignment to Your will, plan and purposes. Let not the plans of man prevail, but let the plans and the purposes of God arise in the land, as well as in our homes. Divine order. We plead the blood over this great land. We plead the blood of Jesus over our families. We thank You for healing arising in this nation. We thank You Your great name, JESUS, is above every name. It is above sickness, above disease, above poverty, shame and misfortune. Your name is great, and greatly to be praised. Pour out YOUR WISDOM. May Godly wisdom and knowledge be our portion.

Reorder our day. Reorder our steps. Reorder our appointments and assignments, calendars and schedules to come into Your perfect order. Let us not miss divine opportunities. Let us not miss divine assignments. Let Your will and Your plan come bursting forth in this land. May God arise and Your enemies be scattered. Our help comes from You Lord.

We thank You we have never seen the righteous forsaken, nor his seed begging bread. There are no beggars in Your kingdom, for we have no want nor lack. Your provisions are always perfect. Even the ravens had purpose, and carried food. Let us weep between the altars and the porch, "spare Your people".

This is the day the Lord has made. May we rejoice and be glad in it. Thank You for covering all connected to or concerning us in the mighty blood of Jesus. Precious is Your name, King Jesus. Bless and protect our children, and our children's children. Thank You our sons and daughters shall prophecy. Old men will dream dreams, and the young men shall see visions. We praise You again this day for being the Great God Jehovah. Mighty is Your name. Let restoration spring forth in the land. May we eat and be satisfied, and praise the name of the Lord.

In Jesus' name, amen.

Your Thoughts and Reflections:

Day 17 with Jesus

15MAR19

Good Morning, Lord…

Was anyone else as excited about the sunshine yesterday as I was?

I wanted to sit in my car and soak it up like a cat in the window!

Praise God for the winds of change blowing in. Blowing out the old. Blowing out the stagnation. Blowing in NEW LIFE. Fresh breath. Fresh wind of God! Breath of God, BLOW!

(Ezekiel 37:9,10) "Also He said to me, 'Prophesy to the breath, prophesy, son of man, and say to the breath, "Thus says the Lord God: 'Come from the four winds, O breath, and breathe on these slain, that they may live.' " So I prophesied as He commanded me, and breath came into them, and they lived, and stood upon their feet, an exceedingly great army.

There's an army rising up! Yes Lord! I thank You that we may speak to the mountains, and they shall move. We shall speak 'breath,' and the wind of God comes! Lord, we speak to these gas prices to come down. We speak to the stagnant pumps, the pumps shut down, oil pumps "PUMP!" "Life come!" "Oil flow!" Make this state LIVE again! "Economy turnaround!" "Wisdom come forth!" Financial WISDOM! "Order come forth!" The order of the Lord."Every crooked place be made straight!" "State come into the order and alignment of the Lord!"

Lord, let us be reminded daily that life and death are in the power of the tongue. Let us speak LIFE. Let us command our day to line up with YOU. Let us speak LIFE into the dry areas, the desolate things, the things seemingly lifeless — that they may LIVE, and not DIE. Restore unto us the JOY of our salvation. RESTORE this land to its original intent. Breath of God, BLOW!

Cover all that is connected to or concerning us in the blood of Jesus. Let the blessings of the Lord chase us down and overtake us; our children & our children's children. We are BLESSED to be a blessing! Kingdom growth, flow and movement come forth!

In Jesus' name, amen.

Your Thoughts and Reflections:

Day 18 with Jesus

23MAR19

Good Morning, Lord…

The Lord is my shepherd. I shall not WANT. That means I have NO LACK. He causes me to lie down in green pastures. That means He gives me rest. Praise God for REST. Good rest. Even though I walk through the valley of the shadow of death, I shall fear no evil. It's merely a walk. Not residence. Amen. He is my comforter and protector. My present help in times of trouble. My rock, my fortress, my strength and strong tower. He is Almighty and all knowing. He is a jealous God, and an all consuming fire. He is mighty to save, and it is not His will that any man should perish. I pray tonight that You know Jesus as your own personal Lord and Savior. If not, repeat after me:

Jesus, thank You for being the Son of God. Who came to this earth and died for ME. Me. Yes, Me. I know that's a lot to comprehend, but God. I confess with my mouth that Jesus is the Christ, the Son of the Living God. I welcome you into my heart. I ask You to be the Lord of my life. Wash me, cleanse me, make me whole and new. Life may not be a cake walk — but as long as I'm walking with the Maker. It is WELL… with my soul.

In Jesus' name, be blessed.

Your Thoughts and Reflections:

Day 19 with Jesus

29MAR19

Good Morning, Lord…

Thank You for FAVOR. Decree with me now:

The FAVOR of the Lord is upon me. The FAVOR of the Lord is upon my house. The FAVOR of the Lord is upon my children & children's children. Favor opens doors. Favor goes before us. Favor is surrounding us. Favor is chasing us down and overtaking us. Glory be to God Most High.

Thank You that GOODNESS and MERCY are following us. Walking with us, throughout our day. Praise God for GOODNESS and MERCY.

Thank You Father that vengeance is not ours, but Yours. Their foot shall slip in due time.

Thank You that obedience is better than sacrifice. It is our obedience that You require. Help us to walk in complete obedience to all You have called us to do.

Thank You that You have a plan. A plan and a purpose for us O Lord. Bless the work of our hands O Lord. Thank You Your word to me was "Prepare to Double Your Numbers." I don't know what exactly that means… but we shall raise a hallelujah, and praise You for a testimony.

(Zechariah 2:8,9) "For thus says the Lord of hosts: 'He sent Me after glory, to the nations which plunder you; for he who touches you touches the apple of His eye. For surely I will shake My hand against them, and they shall become spoil for their servants. Then you will know that the Lord of hosts has sent Me."

(Zechariah 10:6-8) "'I will strengthen the house of Judah, And I will save the house of Joseph. I will bring them back, Because I have mercy on them. They shall be as though I had not cast them aside;

For I am the Lord their God, And I will hear them. Those of Ephraim shall be like a mighty man, And their heart shall rejoice as if with wine. Yes, their children shall see it and be glad; Their heart shall rejoice in the Lord. I will whistle for them and gather them, For I will redeem them; And they shall increase as they once increased."

Somebody shout INCREASE.

(1 Chron.4:10) "And Jabez called on the God of Israel saying, 'Oh, that You would bless me indeed, and enlarge my territory, that Your hand would be with me, and that You would keep me from evil, that I may not cause pain!' So God granted him what he requested."

Lord, bless Your people this day. Cover all connected to or concerning us in the blood of Jesus.

In Jesus' name, amen.

Your Thoughts and Reflections:

Day 20 with Jesus

01APR19

Good Morning, Lord…

May we enter into Your gates with praise, and into Your courts with thanksgiving. Thank You the sun is shining. It is a beautiful day. Thank You the old structures are coming down. The "old" is being thrown out — taken out, moved out, removed. No longer will we hang onto anything not needed — worn out, expired or expended. Thank You for cleaning and clearing — making room for the NEW. Remove all that weighs us down. Remove every distraction. Remove everything that does not line up with the word of God. Stand us back upright, O Lord, that we will no longer remain in a "bent" state. May our faith make us whole.

Lord, keep us on Your schedule. Keep us about Your business. Help us with the "cleaning & clearing" process. May we make room for all You are sending, delivering or bringing to us. Blessed be Your name.

Help us to comprehend — to understand — bring understanding Lord that what You are doing — the NEW — will not look like the old. It will not work the way it once did. Things have to be done differently. Set us on course. Set us on that path — the righteous path You have laid out before us. Lead us not into temptation, but deliver us from evil. Tear down, dismantle the "imposters." Vashti (Esther 1) was removed from being queen when she did not show honor. Adonijah tried to promote himself to the position of king when it was assigned to Solomon. Let the imposters be removed. Let self-promotion have no portion nor residence in our lives.

Lord, there are those appointed and assigned to speak into the lives of kings and leaders. Send the messengers to deliver the word that every wrong seat or position is removed and up-rooted, and every designated, anointed and appointed one is put into their rightful position. Praise God for UPROOTING and REPOSITIONING, In Jesus name.

Bless the work of our hands that we may be fruitful, multiply and subdue the land. Let the double portion fall. Cover all connected to or concerning us in the blood of Jesus. Bless our children & our children's children.

In Jesus' name, amen.

Your Thoughts and Reflections:

Day 21 with Jesus

09APR19

Good Morning, Lord!

Have I told You lately how much I love this sunshine!! Nah, but fa' real! This sunshine tho! Birds singing. Green grass! Be still my heart! Bless the Lord, O my soul! Bless His holy name!

Lord, thank You for ALREADY having our day planned. Thank You that we shall be productive. Thank You for such great revelations You pour out on your children. You are mighty and awesome, Oh God.

Lord, thank You that we are free. Where the spirit of the Lord is, there is freedom. We are no longer slaves. We are no longer bound. We have been set free.

An elephant that has been bound to a chain walking in the same spot — the same circle for so long — stays in that spot, even when the chain has been removed, because it has never realized it is FREE. Lord, thank You our chains have been removed, and we are FREE. Whom the Son sets FREE is FREE INDEED!

Thank You so much, Father God, for setting the captives FREE.

You are great. You are wonderful. You are mighty to save O Lord.

Bless the work of our hands. May we be fruitful, multiply and subdue the land You have given us. Expand our borders. Enlarge the place of our tent. Strengthen our stakes, O Lord. God, You are amazing. Oh, how we love You, O Lord.

Cover all connected to or concerning us in the blood of Jesus.

In Jesus' name, amen.

Your Thoughts and Reflections:

Day 22 with Jesus

04MAY19

Good Morning, Lord…

What a glorious day it is! Blessed are those who dwell together in unity! Let us sing praises to Your name O Lord.

Lord, thank You for delivering us from "Egypt" — the place of bondage, slavery, poverty and lack — not prospering. Help us to recognize the these areas still lingering in our lives. Help us to pluck up, pull down, bind, break, tear down and demolish these strongholds in our lives. Things, people, places that operate in a manner not allowing us to be free, grow or produce. For we know, whom the Son sets FREE is FREE INDEED. Deliver us from the oppressing spirits. Help us to fully recognize those things that cause division, discord, disunity, strife, jealousy, anger, wrath, murder, condemnation, pride, envy, rage, hatred, gossip, slander. Open our eyes and ears to see, hear and recognize these things. Break off every entanglement of such things.

Lord, help us to recognize that which is life giving. Those things which bring or carry peace, joy, prosperity. Let there be no unequal yokes operating in our lives. May we be yoked up with YOUR people. Heading in Your direction. On Your path. May we not be weighted down or attached to life draining sources, activities, individuals or partnerships. Thank You for sending YOUR people to us this day.

Where the enemy has come in one way, may he flee now in seven. Where division has occurred, let unity come forth. Repair the breach O Lord. Set us on Your course. Part the Red Sea that we may march forward. In unity. In step. In step with the Lord. Thank You for those assigned to lead us out. We praise You today for recognition of these sent ones. Recognizing who is FOR us, and who was sent against us. We bless Your holy name.

Cover all connected to or concerning us in the blood of Jesus. Disconnect, unhook everything not of You, O Lord.

In Jesus' name, amen.

Your Thoughts and Reflections:

Day 23 with Jesus

07MAY19

Good Morning, Lord…

It's another beautiful day! Thank You for the sounds of nature. What a blessing to be able to awaken, be still and soak in the sounds. You paint the most beautiful pictures.

(Jude 1:20-25) "But you, beloved, building yourselves up on your most holy faith, praying in the Holy Spirit, keep yourselves in the love of God, looking for the mercy of our Lord Jesus Christ unto eternal life. And on some have compassion, making a distinction; but others save with fear, pulling them out of the fire, hating even the garment defiled by the flesh. Now to Him who is able to keep you from stumbling, And present you faultless Before the presence of His glory with exceeding joy, To God our Savior, Who alone is wise, Be glory and majesty, Dominion and power, Both now and forever, Amen."

Lord, thank You for discernment and recognition. Recognizing those who are "for" us, and those who are "against" us. Against us may merely mean, "not in our best interest." Not sent to build us up, but rather break us down. What might that look like you ask?

Vs.16-19 "These are grumblers, complainers, walking according to their own lusts; and they mouth great swelling words, flattering people to gain advantage. But you, beloved, remember the words which were spoken before the apostles of our Lord Jesus Christ: how they told you that there would be mockers in the last time who would walk according to their own ungodly lusts. These are sensual persons, who cause divisions, not having the Spirit."

Father God, thank You for always keeping Your hand upon us. Sometimes O Lord, you simply save us from ourselves. Thank You for that! Help us to discern that we "can't save the world," but there are those You have sent us to, and assigned us too. Help us to discern the difference. Those who are "for" us. Those who are "against" us. Keep our discernment sharp. We know iron sharpens iron. Guard our hearts. Reveal the true intents. You Alone, Lord, know the intents of the heart. Thank You for that. Thank You for this season of breakthrough upon us. Thank You for plucking the wolves out from amongst the sheep. Keep us on Your path. You Alone make the crooked places straight. Thank You for filling the holes, packing them down, sealing the cracks so we would no longer be leaky vessels. It is by Your strength and power working within us we are made whole.

Bless the work of our hands that we may continue being fruitful, multiplying and subduing the land. Thank You for cutting dead branches, trimming the fat, cutting the wicks. Spring cleaning heavenly Father. Thank You for that.

Cover all connected to or concerning us in the blood of Jesus. Thank You for properly stretching us, that we are able to contain and maintain what we are intended to carry.

In Jesus' name, amen.

Your Thoughts and Reflections:

Day 24 with Jesus

11MAY19

Good Morning, Lord...

Thank You that You, O Lord, ALREADY have our day handled and in Your order. You have appointments, assignments and tasks for us to carry out and complete. You are the TASK MASTER. Creator, Father, Maker, Counselor and King of All. Thank You that Daddy Always Knows Best! Praise the Lord!

Thank You for divine interruptions. Interrupting the plans that are not of You. Interrupting the paths and directions that are not Your purposes and plans for us. Thank You for RESTORED VISION. Clarity in our vision. Wash the windshield of our faith, and cause us to SEE clearly. Clear the path ahead of us.

Thank You for debt reduction. Lightening the load. Lifting off the heavy burdens. YOKE easy. BURDEN light. Setting the captives FREE. For whom the Son sets FREE is FREE indeed. Hallelujah Jesus!

(Jeremiah 33:3) "'Call to Me, and I will answer you and show you great and mighty things which you do not know.'"

Thank You for showing us what we do not know, what we cannot see, what has been hidden — reveal it O Lord. Reveal the hidden things. Reveal the secret things. You know all. You see all. Keep us on the road called STRAIGHT. Keep us on Your schedule. Keep us on Your agenda. Keep our eyes tuned, and our vision sharp and clear. Increase our discernment. Empty us and fill us with MORE OF YOU Lord.

Bless the work of our hands. Bless us indeed. Keep Your hand upon us. Enlarge our territories. May we not cause harm, O Lord. Expose. Reveal. Restore. Wash away the mud. Wash away the dirt and grime. Let the glory of the Lord come forth. Cover all connected to or concerning us in the blood of Jesus.

In Jesus mighty name, amen.

Your Thoughts and Reflections:

Day 25 with Jesus

24JAN21

Good morning, Lord…

As I spent yesterday in a day of rest, much has been on my mind. So many confirmations this day on Jesus' prayer, "Lord, if it be Your will then let this cup pass from me." And He did not.

What happens when He does not let the cup pass from you? You did ask — not my will but THY WILL, and the cup did not pass. Again, perspective — SHIFT your focus. If the Lord did not allow the cup to pass, then truly there is a GREATER PURPOSE; a GREATER ASSIGNMENT at hand. What if we began to pray now: Lord, REVEAL thy greater purpose. Lord, what is my assignment? Lord, for whom can I pray, and how would You have me to pray? Lord, signs, wonders and miracles followed them who believed and acted in Your name. Let signs, wonders and miracles FOLLOW ME, that they may KNOW IT IS YOU. Let us see the GREATER GLORY.

You said, "greater works would we do." Thank You for leaving us THE HELPER. Thank You for our tribe. Order our day. Order our steps. Change, change and rearrange our schedules, appointments and calendars to be set in Your perfect will, that we may not miss any divine appointments. Cover all connected to or concerning us in the mighty blood of Jesus. Bless the work of our hands that we may be fruitful, multiply and subdue the land. Help us to be EFFICIENT, that nothing is wasted. Not time, not energy, not even our words. May we HEAR & SEE more, and SPEAK LESS.

Give us Your eyes, Your ears and be our mouthpiece —

In Jesus' name, amen.

Your Thoughts and Reflections:

Day 26 with Jesus

08APR19

Good Morning, Lord…

Thank You for STRATEGIES. Overcoming STRATEGIES. Breakthrough. Persistence. Pushing through. New Life. New Growth. Things beginning to sprout.

Thank You for taking out the trash. OVERCOMING. Overcoming that which tried to overcome us. Pushing. Pushing. Plowing and pushing.

Thank You for a second wind. Catching our breath. Catching a glimpse. Seeing HOPE again. HOPE on the horizon.

GOSHEN — get us to GOSHEN. The FERTILE land. The place we are able to produce, or be productive, until we can fully exit Egypt. Thank You for FAVOR. UNCOMMON FAVOR. Realignment. Readjusting. Restructuring. Reevaluating. Reordering. A time and place of going back over all that needs shifted, decreased or reworked.

God, You are mighty. You are awesome. You are more than enough, and make all things possible.

You alone are holy, holy, holy. Holy, holy, holy is the Lord God Almighty.

Bless the work of our hands. May we be fruitful, multiply and subdue the land. Thank You for enlarging our tents. Keep Your hand upon us. May we not cause harm, O Lord.

Bless and protect our children, children's children, homes, finances, vehicles, families, jobs & ministries.

In Jesus' name, amen.

Your Thoughts and Reflections:

Day 27 with Jesus

13APR19

Good Morning, Lord!

Thank You for today. Thank You for Your plans and purposes for THIS day. That even THIS day we will walk on the path You have laid out for us. Thank You for YOUR purposes prevailing in our lives. Blessed be Your name, King Jesus.

Thank You for being the true vine. The vine dresser. You prune and take away all that stunts growth, or does not produce. Thank You that as we abide in You, You move and work on our behalf. Lead us this day, O Lord. Guide us this day O Lord. Blessed be Your name.

(John 15:1-8) "'I am the true vine, and My Father is the vinedresser. Every branch in Me that does not bear fruit, He takes away; and every branch that bears fruit He prunes, that it may bear more fruit. You are already clean, because of the word which I have spoken to you. Abide in Me, and I in you. As the branch cannot bear fruit of itself, unless it abides in the vine, neither can you, unless you abide in Me. I am the vine, you are the branches. He who abides in Me, and I in him, bears much fruit; for without Me, you can do nothing. If anyone does not abide in Me, he is cast out as a branch, and is withered; and they gather them and throw them into the fire, and they are burned. If you abide in Me, and My words abide in you, you will ask what you desire, and it shall be done for you. By this My Father is glorified, that you bear much fruit; so you will be My disciples.'"

Lord, may we be bearing much fruit. May it not be rotten, spoiled nor soured. Help us to walk through this with a joyful heart. May sorrow no longer weigh us down. Get us to the place that we are able to produce. Create in us a clean heart. Help us to walk upright before You, O Lord.

Cover all connected to or concerning us in the blood of Jesus. In Jesus' name, amen.

Your Thoughts and Reflections:

Day 28 with Jesus

10FEB21

Good Morning, Lord…

Thank You for this beautiful morning. Thank You for time to pause, reflect and gather what You are saying. Thank You for the revelation You are downloading and pouring out. You never cease to amaze me. Thank You for "re-housing" us. You have continued to speak to me, and confirm Your word about the SOIL. Thank You that my father was a farmer, and my grandmother loved plants, to teach me that GROWTH is dependent on the type of SOIL something is PLANTED in. Growth is also dependent on the nourishment it is provided. Seeds grow in dark places.

Many of us have been in "that dark place," not knowing what was going on. Nevertheless, You sustained us! Glory Hallelujah! Thank You a time and season of REPOTTING / REPLANTING is upon us. Though some have bloomed in adversity, yet failed to see fruit. Some have outgrown their containers, needing more space, and possibly even being root bound. Some need new soil, for they are stuck in a dry place lacking proper nourishment. Nevertheless, You have sustained us up to this point. Thank You for "faith" steps. One step at a time. One day at a time. When we know not what to do, we merely continue to do the next right thing. We praise You for the truth, and those surrounding us speaking truth and LIFE into us. Where light is, darkness cannot remain. Thank You for turning on the lights of Your people.

What might "re-housing" look like? God is in the transformation business.

(2 Corinthians 5:17) "Therefore, if anyone is in Christ, he is a new creation; old things have passed away; behold, all things have become new."

(Jeremiah 29:11-13) "For I know the thoughts that I think toward you, says the Lord, thoughts of peace and not of evil, to give you a future and a hope. Then you will call upon Me, and go and pray to Me, and I will listen to you. And you will seek Me and find Me, when you search for Me with all your heart."

(1 Corinthians 6:12) "All things are lawful for me, but all things are not helpful. All things are lawful for me, but I will not be brought under the power of any."

(Nahum 1:7) "The Lord is good, A stronghold in the day of trouble; And He knows those who trust in Him."

(1 Corinthians 10:12,13) "Therefore let him who thinks he stands take heed lest he fall. No temptation has overtaken you, except such as is common to man; but God is faithful, who will not allow you to be tempted beyond what you are able, but with temptation will also make the way of escape, that you may be able to bear it."

Lord, help us to flee temptations today. Thank You that You always make a way of escape, but it is our choice, our free will, as to whether we take that way or not. We long to bloom. We long to be productive, fully and properly nourished. We want to bear good fruit, for one is known by their fruit. May our fruit be that of the Holy Spirit, and not the flesh.

(Galatians 5:16-26) "I say then: Walk in the Spirit, and you shall not fulfill the lust of the flesh. For the flesh lusts against the Spirit, and the Spirit against the flesh; and these are contrary to one another, so that you do not do the things you wish. But if you are led by the Spirit, you are not under the law. Now the works of the flesh are evident, which are: adultery, fornication, uncleanness, lewdness, idolatry, sorcery, hatred, contentions, jealousies, outbursts of wrath,

selfish ambitions, dissensions, heresies, envy, murders, drunkenness, revelries, and the like; of which I tell you beforehand, just as I also told you in time past, that those who practice such things will not inherit the kingdom of God. But the fruit of the Spirit is love, joy, peace, longsuffering, kindness, goodness, faithfulness, gentleness, self-control. Against such there is no law. And those who are Christ's have crucified the flesh with its passions and desires. If we live in the Spirit, let us also walk in the Spirit. Let us not become conceited, provoking one another, envying one another."

(Galatians 6:6-10) "Let him who is taught the word share in all good things with him who teaches. Do not be deceived, God is not mocked; for whatever a man sows, that he will also reap. For he who sows to the flesh will of the flesh reap corruption, but he who sows to the Spirit will of the Spirit reap everlasting life. And let us not grow weary while doing good, for in due season we shall reap if we do not lose heart. Therefore, as we have opportunity, let us do good to all, especially to those who are of the household of faith."

Lord, help us not to feed our flesh today. Thank You that as You provide our daily bread, the nourishment & provisions for today, it is healthy causing growth, reproduction and multiplication. Thank You for Your kingdom coming, Your will on earth — right here with us right now. May it be here right now as it is in heaven. Right now, we don't have to wait until tomorrow or next week or next year- the kingdom of heaven is at hand — within reach — right now — today. HELP US to GRASP HOLD OF IT, and not let go. Forgive us of our sins. Wash, cleanse, purify our hearts. Lead us not into temptation, but deliver us from the evil one. You are a jealous God, the great God Almighty, righteous, holy, king and counselor. Bless the work of our hands that we may be fruitful, multiplying and subduing the land. Bless and protect our children, and our children's children. Cover everything connected to or concerning us in the mighty blood of Jesus. Continue to change, change and rearrange everything not in accordance or alignment to Your will, Your way, Your time schedule or calendar. REAP-POINT or REASSIGN what is needed or necessary.

In the mighty name of Jesus, amen.

Your Thoughts and Reflections:

Day 29 with Jesus

15APR19

Good Morning, Lord…

Thank You the sun is shining. Lord, help us to be courageous. Help us to be bold. Lead us on Your path. Keep us upright. Thank You our day. Our steps are ordered by You, O Lord. You have divine appointments for us, O Lord. You have divine assignments for us, O Lord. You, Lord, are righteous. You Lord are holy. In You we put our trust. Blessed be Your name, King Jesus.

Thank You again for overcoming strategies. Lay out Your blueprints. Help us to remain focused, goal oriented and moving forward with intent as well as purpose. Help us to not miss the mark, Lord. Help us to remember we can do ALL things in and through You. You, Lord cause us to be MORE THAN CONQUERORS. Our God is mighty to save. Our God is able. With You, O Lord. All things are possible.

In Jesus' name, amen.

(Philippians 4:13) "I can do all things through Christ who strengthens me."

Your Thoughts and Reflections:

_____

_____

_____

Day 30 with Jesus

28MAR19

Good Morning, Lord…

(Psalm 138:3) "In the day when I cried out, You answered me, And made me bold with strength in my soul."

(vs.7,8) "Though I walk in the midst of trouble, You will revive me; You will stretch out Your hand Against the wrath of my enemies, And Your right hand will save me. The Lord will perfect that which concerns me; Your mercy, O Lord, endures forever; Do not forsake the works of Your hands."

Let us raise a hallelujah…for the Lord will perfect that which concerns us. What an awesome word that is.

Father, thank You for today. Thank You for the Song of Solomon 2:11,12: "For lo, the Winter is past, The rain is over and gone. The flowers appear on the earth; The time of singing has come, And the voice of the turtledove Is heard in our land."

Lord, let us sing with a new song on our lips. One of LOVE. One of FORGIVENESS. One of PARDON — pardoning iniquities. Forgiving the wrongs others have done to us. Forgiving what we ourselves have done. Let us sing with a new song. Blessed be Your name. Let us sing a song of RESTORATION, REBUILDING and NEW GROWTH. Let us sing a song of things sprouting forth. Ground breaking. Multiplication. Let us till the ground, and begin to sow our seed for harvest. Let shame no longer have it's portion. Let rejection be stamped null and void — rejected. Because You Lord are the one who PERFECTS US. Let all deceit and malice be thrown out and burned away for You O Lord are an all consuming fire and a jealous God. Thank You that whatever You have joined together man is not able to set asunder. Let UNITY have its portion. For blessed are those who dwell together in unity.

(Psalm 149:1) "Praise the Lord! Sing to the Lord a new song, And His praise in the assembly of saints."

vs.4-6 "For the Lord takes pleasure in His people; He will beautify the humble with salvation. Let the saints be joyful in glory; Let them sing aloud on their beds. Let the high praises of God be in their mouth, And a two-edged sword in their hand."

Lord, thank You for going before us today and setting our day in Your order. Thank You for unclogging, unblocking & unstopping all that was bound. Thank You for releasing the flow. Bless the work of our hands that we may be fruitful, multiply and subdue the land. Cover all connected to or concerning us in the blood of Jesus.

In Jesus' name, amen.

Your Thoughts and Reflections: